Dynamo Memory

Dynamo Memory

poems by
Paul Archer

Matador
9 Priory Business Park,
Wistow Road, Kibworth Beauchamp,
Leicestershire. LE8 0RX
Tel: 0116 279 2299
Email: books@troubador.co.uk
Web: www.troubador.co.uk/matador
Twitter: @matadorbooks

ISBN 978 1789010 244

British Library Cataloguing in Publication Data.
A catalogue record for this book is available from the British Library.

Printed and bound in the UK by 4edge limited
Typeset in 11pt Minion Pro by Troubador Publishing Ltd, Leicester, UK

Matador is an imprint of Troubador Publishing Ltd

for
Mike and Debbie

Contents

Lemons on the Lemon Trees	1
Summer in Mallorca	2
Gardener's Friend	3
Sunset Swim at Bens d'Avall	5
Encounter with a Blackbird	6
Memories of Japan	9
I Rose Garden	9
II Namari Spa	10
III Cherry Blossom Viewing	11
IV Okinawa	12
What I Wear for Writing	13
Nairobi Conference	14
2:45 am the Wind	15
Snowy Morning	16
Snail's Pace	18
Meeting Geoff in the Plaza	19
Loose-lace Shoes	20
The Solicitude of Solitude	22
Keep Off The Grass	23
The Poems Project	24
Callers	25
Archer River	27
Stunned by Shakespeare	28
A Little Italian Place	30
Flatpack Poem	32
Advice to Poets	33
She Sang	35
Goring-by-Sea	36
Snap	38
Crazy Golf	40

The First Eleven 42

Running Shoes 44

Ars Moriendi 46

Dynamo Memory 48

Lemons on the Lemon Trees

Lemons like lanterns in the trees,
tired green leaves, darkening sky.

Not the lemons money can buy:
not icy yellow, smooth and pristine;
these are swollen-bellied, knobby,
blotched cream, ochre, green,
pores like magnified human skin.

Battle-hard veterans, rough outlaws;
wild beasts that can't be corralled;
survivors of frenzied African winds
belting through, buckling their stems,
blasting their skin with Saharan sand.

This evening as the coolness descends
they glow like lanterns in the trees.

Summer in Mallorca

The terrace stripped bare of every shadow.
A gecko basks. The sun sheers off
dimensions and desiccates
the orange trees' leaves, the soil, their roots.
A dictatorship blaring senseless
propaganda through klaxon sunrays.
A herrador in a ferocious forge
hammering on the anvil of the earth,
banging flat the detail of wisdom and words.

And we long for the days of limpidness,
the torrente running through melting green,
frost-fresh air, the delicate peony petals.
This is when humankind expires:
yes, there's the stabbing chill of winter
to gouge the you from you, the me from me;
but summer heat's a smiling assassin
skilled in the snake's deceiving arts
as it moves to the kill, softening, stroking.

We return to the house's shaded rooms,
the custom-bound particulars of daily life
with the sun's silent scream at the windows,
carrying something to show that out of endurance
some good may come, owing its very being
to the suffering: a basket of ripe oranges
for slicing, for squeezing out the tangy syllables
of a language that will come to us in dreams
hanging from limp green-leafed boughs.

Gardener's Friend

Sweat filmed my spectacles as I forked the soil
ready for vegetables to sow from packs of seed

wiping the glasses on my shirt and replacing them,
I saw a robin on the earth looking around, taking a step,
pecking in mimicry

a robin at the apex of a lineage of robins,
like me in that, and also that we both
were on a mission to find sustenance from the earth
like all that grew around us

I could have pitied the robin
for what it was missing out on:
that it would never have a bank account,
hopefully full of money,
or dress up for a party or go to a concert
or visit an art gallery
or send its fellows to that round white thing
that hangs in the branches of the night sky

but I could see it didn't pity or envy me
for if I left off working the wild weeds would come back
and a wilderness would be no good for me
but would make no difference to a robin

it darted its eye from me down to what it was there for
and all was right about its simplicity

I hefted my fork again,
digging with vigour in each downward push,

a new rhythm in each turning of the tines
and what their pecking brought forth from the soil

thinking as a robin might
of when I'm through
with this back-breaking ground-breaking toil
and return to rest
in the nest
I'd
fly
up to

Sunset Swim at Bens d'Avall

We only went
to the bay
at Bens d'Avall
to freshen
sticky skin
cleanse
dusty heads
with bristling
coolness -
what we got
was a swim
on a brassy path
to orange flares
in white clouds,
fan-blades of purple,
shangri-las of powdery blue

this extravaganza
from the hand of nature
can only be counterfeited
by the hand of man
in the words on a page,
the lights and smoke
of a Vegas stage

what we saw gave more
than just by looking
we could ever see

Encounter with a Blackbird

Once - while pruning orange trees,
snipping white wood
out of lime-green leaves -
I saw a cluster of dead twigs
and stepped up the ladder,
secateurs raised,
and there: a sleek head,
yellow beak, rivet eye.

That night I dreamt
she sat on silver foil
and not with eggs, but potatoes
warm and butter-slippery.
I turned them for her
and stuck them in a pan
to roast in an oven.
Can you eat your own dreams?

Cool before-dawn air slipped in
bringing an orange blossom breeze
and a limpid arpeggio of notes.
She had got into my dreams.
Was I in hers?

Mangling into myth
the shock of a giant
rearing out of nowhere,
moon-faced, stark-eyed,
jutting out a mandible
with sharp-cutting jaws,

the don't-move imperative
countering the instinct
to flee into safe sky
as her glossy-feathered
lineage chills
to lifeless shells.

Hunching over these words
like new-laid eggs,
hearing each whistled quaver
tumbling proudly
from the orange tree,
I listened like never before.

Her song called up the sun.
It tilted over the hill and rolled
blazing down the valley's slope,
and so I left my words
to fester in their nest,
and stepped onto the terrace
above the orange grove

crushed by the racket
of cars, vans and trucks,
clanking construction machinery,
the fevered rush of money
as it whistles from this
to that, and, scanning the trees,
remembered how,

once, our shared space
shrunk to levelled eyes,
astounded, fearful,
fighting and cowed,
and then widened
to a respectable distance.

We were humbled, yet
full of the same pride
as when lovers meet, then part,
and will never meet again
and are wise.

Memories of Japan

I

Rose Garden

I strain to catch the words
of the roses, however
much I draw inwards
their scent and colour.

I've listened too long
to the frenetic fountain
bursting into airy song,
stippling the pool's skin.

I've lost my senses
in the carp's stealth,
circling upon itself
within its absences.

Fukuyama, 1981

II

Namari Spa

The waterfall mimics the noise
of brittle-winged cicadas.

The river's slurred vowels
trip tipsily through the stones.

The maples wave across the gorge
as if their leaves know each other.

III

Cherry Blossom Viewing

I
High-kicking can-can dancers
reveal their blossom's lace.

My feet plod the pathway
but I don't feel their steps.

II
Cherry blossom drifts down
on the young girls drifts down

Their skin is as white as petals
cherry blossom drifts down

III
Under the cherry trees
drinking saké.

White petals,
red faces.

IV

Okinawa

Tan legs tie and untie bows
in streams of striped fish.

Gliding down veils of pinks
and reds, the white sun goes...

Crabs pincer up the sand,
clatter discarded Coca-Cola cans.

What I Wear for Writing

Sometimes I write naked
as a Neanderthal.
I write about bones and fire.
Or I'll put on the cumbersome
suit of an astronaut
and write about emptiness.
When the subject's sex
I find that a dinner jacket
and purple beret does the trick.
What am I wearing now, you ask.
It might be that black mask,
sailor's cap and bullet-proof vest
that I wear to formal occasions
like weddings, regattas
and the State Opening of Parliament.
Or it could simply be my favourite
t-shirt with the boldly printed slogan:
"I am your creation".
But I'd rather keep you guessing.
I have to leave something
to your imagination.

Nairobi Conference

In the comfort of its air-conditioned chamber
the conference faces up to climate change
by deploying words like 'urgent' and 'action'.

Two hours away, the Masai are surviving
on their own, fighting their hunger, losing
their cattle in drought after drought.

The Swaziland dancers and drummers
perform on the conference hotel's lawn
in front of stiff lines of suited delegates.

A smell of beef hits their nostrils
and thick smoke wafts over from a barbecue
of useless and worthless press releases.

6 -17 November, 2006

2:45 am the Wind

Tugging and tearing -
backing off - tugging and tearing,
but this is not a terrier.

It's the wind punching at ghosts,
arguing with itself, railing against
the air it's forced to live in.

Stalking out - silence - back again.
So back from the past
come bellowing visions.

With restless appetite we
gnaw at the knuckle of our history,
sharpening teeth for conflicts,

or grinding them flat and useless,
senseless as a rattling house,
as mindless as a banging window.

On a starless night like this
with the wind's noise blowing through it,
with the world's noise blowing through it,

we are the restless ones,
kept safe from the buffeting
storm by roofs and walls, but not from

what tugs and tears
and will not leave off, even
in the morning's silent stillness.

Snowy Morning

Have you taken a grapefruit from the fridge,
sliced it open, segmented it with the serrated knife,
sprinkled sugar on, while stood at the kitchen window
startled by the first winter snowfall?
Staring into the chilled and crowded air
the tang of the grapefruit smacks
its truth onto your tongue and throat
as it slips down, slice by slice.

Last night the bald trees were brown,
the grass in patches, the bushes clipped back.
The glamour of snow has bewitched the silent birds
and the boy that runs from the back door
in gum boots, hat askew, jacket unbuttoned,
and mother yelling him back, who stops only
to open wide his eyes and mouth, arms
and fingers, to the crystal flakes.

He feels he's happened on a fairy tale's
deliverance from darkest sleep;
while we, grown older, see the world's shift
as news, like any other unexpected event
that makes the news. We think of slippery paths,
frozen cars, cold knees and necks
and the inconvenience of ice; we shiver
and switch the coffee machine on.

But did something touch us
slithering like a soft feather falling into
the spaces between words? And were those words
like bells chiming in the crystal air?

Then let each day be like a snowy morning,
even your last on earth, as your spoon delves
again into the grapefruit, its juices
dissolving the sprinkled sugar snow to slush.

Snail's Pace

It had climbed from the lavender
under the open window
and now creeps along the sill.
I think of Hughes' thought-fox
and Lowell's skunk,
then slow down…

slow down; for a creature
moving so slowly the world
flashes by too fast… now my feelers
probe tentatively, I heave
myself over the minutest obstacles
leaving a silvery trace…

Then my godlike hand plucks the snail
from the sill and tosses it out -
'Don't even think about living in MY house
without paying the rent!'
In that attitude, also, it may be said
that I am godlike.

Meeting Geoff in the Plaza

I don't have to sit there long
before someone I know
stops to have a coffee with me,
it's that kind of plaza
with café tables under trees,

and now Geoff
swings by and we get
to talk about his latest work,
his painting of a suicide bombing in a café
and how people were chatting there one moment and the next
were just… burnt meat, and what was it that had gone? I don't see
how he can get all this into a painting, but I'm sure Geoff does.
Art has a way of taking us out of ourselves and out of time.
But these days, as Geoff now says, it's astonishing how little time
people spend looking at a painting in an art gallery,
even a Renoir. Can a poem get more attention?
Maybe less… in any case, here's Geoff,
pulling up his chair next to mine,
catching the waiter's eye, making
his debut in a poem,

a poem that's like a café table
in a plaza, where anyone
can hang out and take their time
before getting on with their day,
and not get blown away.

Loose-lace Shoes

Here's what happened on my way home
not half an hour ago: the shoelace
came undone on one of my shoes,
the right one. I heard it ticking,
its ends flicking on the pavement,
I saw it arcing with each step,
bobbing, cartwheeling, somersaulting.
I should've stopped to pull it tight
and thread it into a bow and fastened
the bow upon itself to make sure,
but out of laziness, or not wanting to
break my flow or make an obstacle
in the path of others, or for whatever reason,
I kept on walking and added an extra
unaccustomed dimension to a familiar walk.
For my right foot felt freer and freer,
as if it were easing itself into another life,
as if it were a bare foot sinking into sand,
or an Indian tracker's on a wild trail,
though, as it was only the right foot,
I was only halfway there – but still…

I paused at a crossing's light, a lady
nodded her head down: "Your shoelace…"
"Oh," feigning surprise and shame
as if caught half-naked rather than
merely half-shod, I bent to tie the lace.
Now I felt the shoe pinching me tight,
squeezing my foot to its shape,
fettering my freedom, for I had
taken on the character of that shoe,

all strait-laced, sensible, dusty and dull,
just like anyone else on the street that day,
or rather, now, not like Someone.
So when your shoelace next springs loose
let it stay that way for a while,
be the only shoelace-loose stranger
on the street, or in the whole town,
and if anyone dares to point and say
that your shoelace is undone,
don't bend down. Look them straight
in the eye, with your head held high,
and reply: "You know what, I like it that way."

The Solicitude of Solitude

If this sun were smoke it would be a shawl
spread between the olive trees, if the trees were gazelles

they'd be perched on graceful legs of frosted dew
but the sun is beaten bronze,
the olive leaves are silver chalices,

and now it was then, and then it was now,
in this hammock slung across the sun between the clouds

Deià, 2012

Keep Off The Grass

Your tour begins in the gallery
with its paintings of long forgotten vistas:
Arabian deserts, English pastures,
Asian rice-fields, Alpine meadows,
American prairies stretching to the horizon.

Now continue through to our museum
and its exhibition of rare specimens
of richly grained oak, sandalwood and pine
from trees that once flourished here on Earth
preserved for your grandchildren's children!

Gaze in awe at our amazing floral show;
each flower has been carefully replicated
from archive drawings with complete accuracy.
Visit our shop to buy a flower to take home,
each has its own particular perfume!

Before you go, don't miss the pride of our collection:
a patch of real, yes, real green grass growing
in a glass cabinet in perfect atmospheric conditions
with miniature clouds producing rain at timed intervals.
Chairs are provided for contemplation.

The Poems Project

The poems project will provide
a capability for the parallel or distributed
implementation of adaptive applications,

using a multi-semiotic language
for composition from personal workloads
to large-scale memory hierarchies.

Resolution will range from large grain
data flows to instructional streams,
from the probabilistic to the deterministic.

Development will concentrate on areas
of unconventional wisdom capable of being
adapted to complex communication systems,

with reliable and varied, multi-dimensional,
subjective, psychophysical and behavioural
measurement methods for perception.

The project will produce poems optimised
to be compact, quiet, low cost and safe
without any potentially damaging moving parts.

Callers

When he comes
hot-footing it up the drive
in those army boots that go so well
with his camouflage jacket,
will there be a polite rap
or a heavy thump on the door?
Or will he just breeze in?
Or perhaps, that day,
it'll be the raven-haired
and sparkly eyed
Contessa de Mort
who whisks you off
into the night where,
at some glittering reception,
she'll hang lovingly on your arm
and gaze deep into your troubled eyes.

Or neither of them.
Maybe it's more like
diving down to a girl
shrieking to be saved
from storm-crushed rocks,
or an eager boy beckoning
from the end of a sandy lane.

Or an elderly man in a stained
yellow waistcoat who murmurs
'Well, that's that then,'
as his wife snaps her spectacles
back into their case and her
cracked lips whisper
'It's time to go.'

Or none of them. No more
than standing looking out to sea
on a headland that crumbles,
one foot on land
one foot in air

and you're not there.

Archer River

When dreams take you somewhere
it's never as good when you get there.

It was just sand and a sluggish red
current with crocs on the bend,

but I had to wade into the water
of the Archer River in Australia,

in Far North Queensland, far
from a schoolboy's inky finger

tracing its course on an atlas
in a dusty schoolroom in Sussex.

So years later I kept my promise.
But I wouldn't want to go there twice,

it's never as good when you get there
when dreams take you somewhere.

Stunned by Shakespeare

I look up to these famous poets,
their books wedged tightly
into shelves that tower above me,
and reach to pull one of them from the top,

it dislodges the others,
the bookcase rocks, books fall out,
slim volumes slide free,
the thin edges of paperbacks
by Gunn and McGough
rain glancing blows,
hardbacks by Auden and Eliot
land head-butts,
then come the thudding tomes
of Pope, Milton, Dryden,
and now – oh no! –
the six pound, three inch thick
Arden Shakespeare Complete Works
bangs down flooring me

I curse you, William.
Why didn't you quit the quill
after those youthful sonnets?
Enough, surely, for immortality.
Why didn't you go out to a dark tavern,
to a loose-hipped wench
begging you to forget the pile
of blank verse-less parchment
on your lonely desk?
Why didn't you listen to the voices
telling you to go back to Stratford,
to Anne, to your family?

Why not be a glover like your father,
they would have said,
people will always need gloves.

Why did you have to be so dome-headed,
so beetle-browed, so prolific a writer?
I rub my bruised head and curse you,
William Shakespeare, whoever you were.

A Little Italian Place

In our hearts we all have that little Italian place
where Luigi ushers us to our favourite corner table
with murals of grapes on the ochre walls
and perhaps signed photos of celebrities
that few have ever heard of
and which anyway can't be seen
as the only light comes from a candle
in a raffia-wrapped Chianti bottle
making a halo where we sit like two saints

here love is simply to be enjoyed and not argued over,
especially when there are more important matters to debate
like whether to have the Tagliatelle or Linguine,
the Valpolicella or Pinot Grigio,
before the world fades beyond the candle's glow,
the shining eyes, the whispers, the gentle touch of fingers.
It would be churlish, crass and rude
to allow even one cross word,
for if that were to ever happen
it seems the waiters would stagger backwards
in astonishment, falling over tables
as the restaurant floor collapses
and its walls slide away into the distance…
It would then be a very large Italian place

but not tonight. No, tonight we've tasted zabaglione
as simply sweet as first love, we've been cosseted
in the cradle of the candle's glow,
then helped into coats and out into the night air,
leaving Luigi, the moustachioed ringmaster of romance,
to set the scene for the next performance:

he straightens the chairs, unfurls a new tablecloth,
crisp and white, and places in the centre a candle
and a vase with a single red rose.

Flatpack Poem

If this poem came from IKEA
it would be a flatpack poem
you'd have to assemble
from its various parts
connecting the metre and rhyme
aligning the alliteration
and offering up heartfelt emotion
and deep thought,
bolting them together
with an Allen key that isn't
yet lost, but will be.
You'd look at the diagrams
but won't figure them out
and you'll see how it goes
by yourself and that's
what we call free verse.
If this poem came from IKEA
it would have an obscure
and even unpronounceable title
like "Norråker" or "Lövbacken"
or "Svartåsen" perhaps,
and we'd all have a poem
somewhere around the house
that was exactly the same
as everybody else's
but pretend we hadn't.

Advice to Poets

Don't drive a car. Dreaming up a poem
is not compatible with judging
distances and steering straight.

Live as long as you can. But think
about dying, the dark mystery
of death will add depth to your poems.

Don't make decisions. Rethink
all the time - you, more than most, should
know we are all flotsam on a great river.

Don't disengage. Live usefully,
greet your neighbour, be warm to those
you write about - they are your readers.

Don't fall in love with the Muse. It will only
create trouble. Write about happiness -
being unhappy is a crowded market.

Write and then re-write. Even if the poem
takes years, make it seem like it took
only the seconds it takes to read.

Anyone can write if they have the time
and will, but most prefer the hassle of living
to the hassle of words - that's a comforting thought.

Be precise, like surgeons or lawyers.
Desire, also, to re-shape the world
as fundamentally as scientists or soldiers.

Make your writing seem like no-one else's,
for that you'll have to ignore any advice
given to you - so you can ignore all I've said.

She Sang

She sang: like no bird has sung
higher than a snowy peak
her voice in the clear air
clearer than air

She sang: like no-one has sung
for words were taken
beyond words to
words not heard before

She sang: like her voice was light
all light and alight
and we all sang with her
(although we didn't sing)

She sang: like her song was spun
into whirling rings
of the all inside all there is
for as long as

she sang

Goring-by-Sea

In the back seat of the Ford Cortina
we jump up and down
playing I-Spy
and First to See the Sea,
a glimpse of greyness
behind skeletal pine trees

Mr Whippy hands
us strawberry mivvis
from the window in his van,
their slick red coats
drip sticky blood over our fingers

in a camp of towels
and folding chairs on the
cannon-ball round pebbles
behind a breakwater
we take cover from the
wind's barrage

over the ribbed sand
of no-man's land we walk
to the sea's sting on the toes,
the wade out and the brave
breath, then the plunge into steely cold

we run back on numbed legs
to a brisk towel-down,
the shell-shock shivering
comforted by thermos tea
and salmon paste sandwiches

the sea claws its way back,
slipping quietly over the sand,
then massing in wave after wave
to mount its assault on the shingle

we fling useless stones into the breakers
thunderously detonating on the beach,
deafened by the bombardment
we fall back

and are brought home,
silent and still
in the back of the Cortina,
dead to the world.

Snap

Do I know who he is,
this freckle-faced lad
standing with a beach
ball on the wet sand?

His striped shirt tucked
into a snake-clasped
multi-coloured belt
on grey flannel shorts,

he poses for the camera
held by my father
in this holiday snap
from where? from when?

From the lost past
of me as I was then,
but I can't find
myself in him and

if he threw the ball
far into the future
for me to catch
it would be snapped

away by the wind
in the time it takes
to reach my hands
and go bounding off

down the long beach,
each bounce lower
than the one before,
until it fetches up

on a barrier of sharp
rocks where it stops,
pricked by a spike,
and slowly deflates.

Crazy Golf

One balmy summer's evening
by the seaside when I was nine,

we hit balls round barriers,
down chutes, through the gates
of fantasy castles,
anything to make torturous
the crooked course
with its tin flags from 1 to 18.

That night I woke
but wasn't really awake
crying from deep in a dream
'It won't go in!'
not understanding the words
until after they came out
only the desperate bursting of shame.

Those words, that cry, that bawl
was putted into the back
of my mind and is there still
as I size up the next hole
on life's miniature course,
designed by someone,
one presumes, to test and amuse.

Then I take a swing
and send the ball rolling away...
all I can do is trust
it's got the luck, line and length
to pass the hazards in its path,
not get stuck in a trap
and not go too slow or too fast,

the balls nears its target,
it rolls round and round the hole,
will it drop now?
- it won't go in! – or will it? -

The First Eleven

The blue and white striped football jersey
plucked from the peg was more chilly
than our own skins as we shrugged it on.
We would clatter out, boot studs grating
on gravel, to the field and the first kicks
of a ball that sucked the grass's wetness
into its leather panels and bumped along
reluctantly, a dead weight against the boot,
and, if not avoided by ducking, the head.

Here's the First Eleven team photograph,
the year 1969 painted on the ball in white,
with five boys seated on schoolroom chairs
and six standing behind, all in striped jerseys
except for the one in an over-large sweater,
the only one allowed to handle the ball,
and so he holds the ball in this photograph
firmly in his hands, the goalie who let in
more goals than we ever got close to scoring.

That was decades ago and those still alive
fear for their knees if a ball hits their foot
and have now set their eyes on the walk back,
but not to a communal shower of tepid water
and a consoling mug of cocoa in the hall,
nor to a class of history or double maths
and gazing blankly out of barred windows
or scoring their name into an ink-stained
wooden desk with a crooked compass point.

Archer, Blackburn, Dizer, Leggatt, Lempicki,
Priestley-Cooper, Turner... legends to ourselves,
at half-time we'd suck orange quarters and gather
round Mr Fox who sat on a shooting stick
and blew acrid smoke from his cigar to disguise
the disaster to come in the second half.
Schooled to take on the world and do our best,
and then greet failure with humour and grace,
we look proudly out of the First Eleven photograph.

Running Shoes

In the early hours the pain came
and she told him now was the time,
so he dashed down the stairs
to his spiked running shoes
ready by the door and ran as fast
as he had ever run in his life
past houses sleeping in the mist
and all he could see was her face,
her anxious face, resolutely braced
against the agony of giving birth.

At the top of the road he rapped
on the midwife's door, then again.
No light came on, no voice replied.
Frantic now, his blood pounding
- should he stay there or go back -
he spun in his shoes this way and that.
Then he spied a pinhead of light
drawing closer through the mist
resolving to his relief into a lamp
as the midwife pedalled up to him.

That was the night when I was born
and I think of it now as I pull on
my Nike trainers to go for a run,
how different the world was then
before telephones in every home
and long before smart phones
reached you at any time or place,
when all you could do was run
up the road for a midwife to come,
as my father did as he ran for my life.

Now I set off and the blood pumps
through my veins, the air thumps
into my lungs, and like a newborn
my eyes awaken and sharpen
the world into focus, and then
I can't stop, I run over the horizon,
and the great ball of the Earth
with its whirling blues and greens
becomes a boy's marble that spins
away from under my shoes as I run on.

Ars Moriendi

Black out. So black
we have to make light of it,
but there's no light,
no touch, taste,
sound, scent – no-one.

How tempting
the temple's rolling song,
honeyed promises
of more to come –

Death crashes into cells,
crumples brains,
chills to the core.
Rot rampages,
gases spew,
flesh ferments,
busy beetles
and filthy flies
strip skin and sinew

from the bones
of those we knew,
the much-prized curves,
the flashlight nerves,
and those who want death
to crush their cares;
all cut down
to a silhouette,
then static, silence.

White out. That winter's
white after the dying
back, making way
for the first cry,
the first stretch of wings.

The blackbird tells us
as she trills from her nest
on a summer's night
that this is all there is.

Her being thrums
as she thrusts
each note into the air,
her song resounds
through our cells,
stirs in our blood
our shared ancestry
and aspiration,
teetering on a toe

over lifelessness...
in the ever-expanding
flux of gas and mass
and immense darkness,
we are a miraculous
spark in the dark;
but we can say
we had our chance.
We had our chance.

Dynamo Memory

My bike's lamp peers ahead
a few yards. Knees pump
under a plastic rain cape.
Tyres swish over tarmac.
Flicking the Sturmey-Archer
lever to the lowest gear,
standing to push the pedals,
zig-zagging the front wheel
up Imberhorne Lane.

I alone can have this memory
not some other boy, his sodden
school cap cutting into his brow,
coasting now as the star-constellation
of East Grinstead rises above the fields.
The recollection comes and goes
like the power from the bike's dynamo.
If I pause, the light glimmers down.
The harder I push, the more the lamp shines.